CALEB THE GREAT: TOUCHDOWN IN NEW ORLEANS

WRITTEN BY CORNEAL WESTBROOKS
ILLUSTRATIONS BY JANINE CARRINGTON

"Caleb the Great: Touchdown in New Orleans" by Corneal Westbrooks
Cover design and illustrations by Janine Carrington

© 2024 CodeWest

Published by CodeWest Books
ISBN 979-8-218-35035-2

All rights reserved. No part of this publication may be reproduced, distributed, or transmitted in any form or by any means, including photocopying, recording, or other electronic or mechanical methods, without the prior written permission of the publisher, except in the case of brief quotations embodied in critical reviews and certain other noncommercial uses permitted by copyright law. For permission requests, write to the publisher, addressed "Attention: Permissions Coordinator," at the address below.

CodeWest Books Chicago
contactcodewest@gmail.com

To my beautiful niece—although you will not be able to develop memories of Caleb for yourself, I am writing this book so you will still know his story.

To my son—I am writing this book to ensure that your memory lives on.

About this story...

I never planned to be a father, but I tried my best. For fifteen years, I did everything within my power to raise my son "right." I was convinced that if he was good, he would be rewarded in some way.

Along our journey, I tried my best to provide him with the knowledge needed to navigate life and avoid its pitfalls. I encouraged him to try new things along the way and to be not only the best at what he chose to do but the happiest.

In the end, I hope he was happy. It took years to come up with the right words needed to properly share his story and it is my wish that his story has a positive impact on someone one day.

PELÉ

In the Windy City of Chicago, a young boy named Caleb lived with his dad. They were best friends, sharing their love of video games, sports, good food, and unforgettable moments together.

One day, Dad surprised Caleb with exciting news; they were moving to the Big Easy, New Orleans.

"What about my friends?" Caleb asked. Caleb was immediately filled with apprehension, because Chicago was the only home that he had ever known.

But he trusted his dad, so he packed his bags and began to imagine what this new city had in store for him and what adventures awaited.

In New Orleans, Caleb's ears were greeted with Jazz music and his nose was introduced to the aroma of Creole cooking. The energy from the locals was contagious.
Caleb's eyes sparkled as they walked through the streets and for the first time, he saw a streetcar whiz by.

His dad smiled. "First off, they don't talk funny. What you hear is a southern accent. Heck, to them, you might sound funny."

He told Caleb, "New Orleans is famous for its culture, delicious food, and love of football, more specifically the home team, the Saints."

As they settled into their new home, Caleb began to notice a group of kids playing football in the park.

Their fun and excitement echoed through the air, and Caleb's curiosity grew.

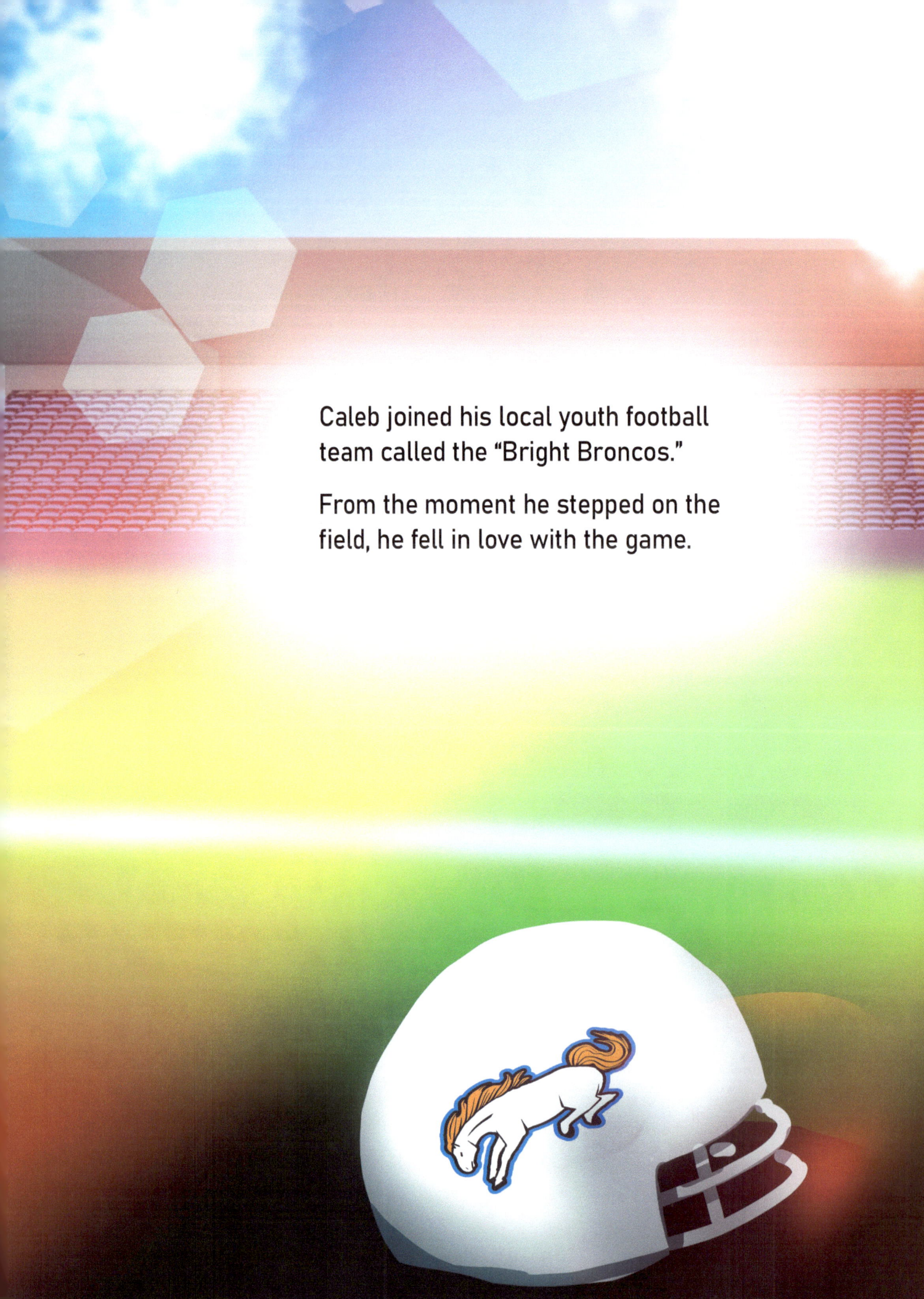

Caleb joined his local youth football team called the "Bright Broncos."

From the moment he stepped on the field, he fell in love with the game.

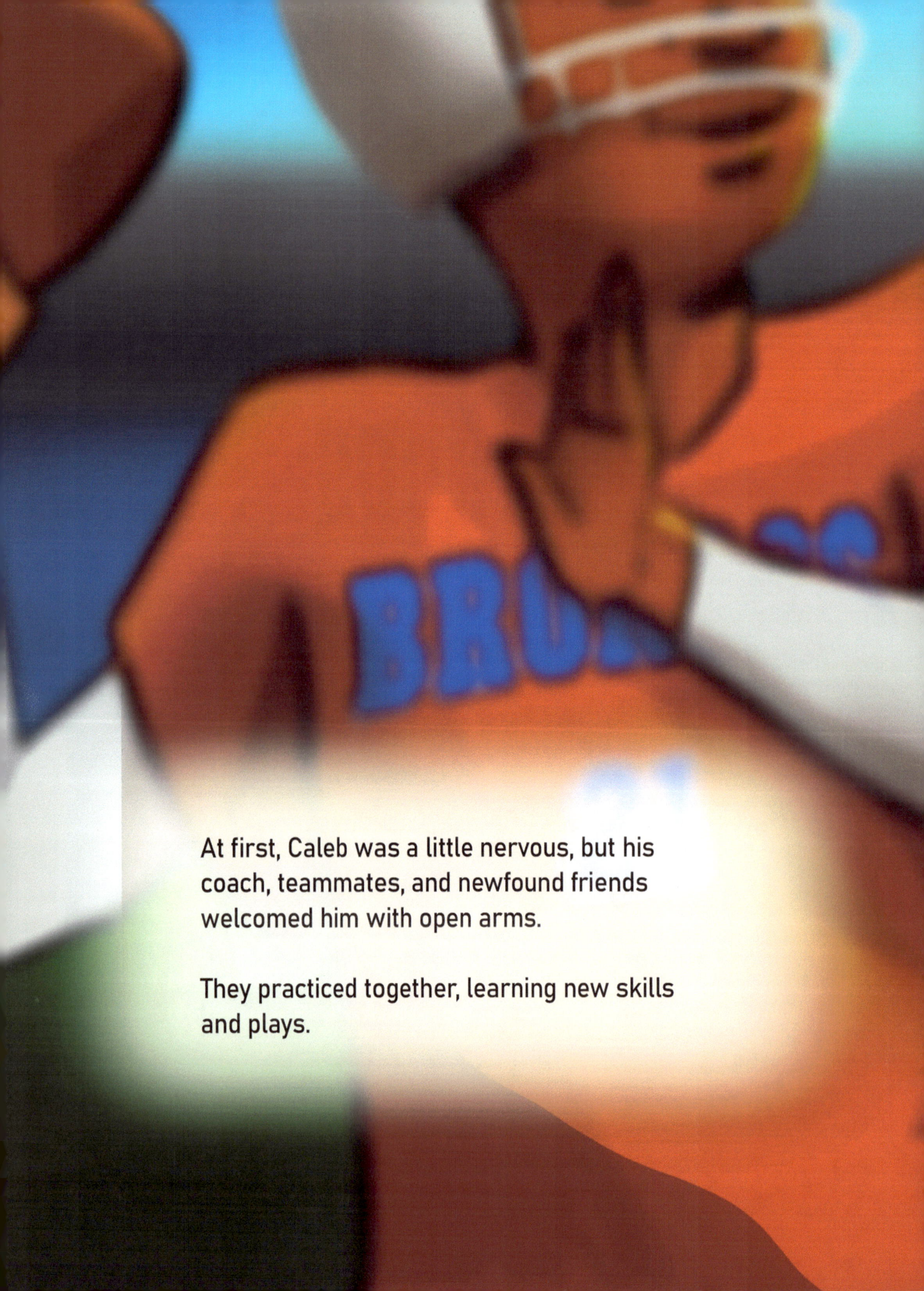

At first, Caleb was a little nervous, but his coach, teammates, and newfound friends welcomed him with open arms.

They practiced together, learning new skills and plays.

Coach Hall was patient and encouraging, and he believed in Caleb's potential.

Running, catching, and scoring touchdowns gave him thrills like nothing else. Caleb's heart raced with every play.

"You've got the heart of a champion, Caleb. Keep working hard and you'll shine on the field," Coach Hall said with a smile.

As the weeks passed, Caleb's skills improved. He felt like a football star, living his dream on the field.

"Dad, I love football! I want to be like Justin Jefferson or Ja'Marr Chase," Caleb said, his eyes shining with determination.

His dad beamed with pride.
"I'm convinced you can be whatever you want to be with a little hard work and determination.
I'm not just saying that because you're my son—I've watched you play and you really are good."

Caleb's team entered a local football tournament.

It was the big day and the stadium was filled with cheering fans.

Caleb's heart raced as he sat in the locker room. His dad smiled at him and said, "You will be just fine. It's your time to shine."

Caleb smiled, grabbed his helmet, and raced onto the field.

With each play, Caleb gave it his all. He made fantastic catches, dodged defenders, and scored touchdowns with relative ease.

The crowd erupted into cheers, and Caleb felt an overwhelming sense of pride. Caleb could see his dad in the crowd cheering him on and that made him play even harder.

In the end, the Bright Broncos won the tournament, and Caleb's obsession with the game grew.

"That's my boy, I'm so proud of you," his dad said. He gave Caleb a high five and grabbed him to hug him tightly.

And so, Caleb's football journey continued, fueled by passion, hard work, and the love and support of his dad. With every touchdown, he knew that he was living a dream that had taken flight in the vibrant city of New Orleans.

For in the world of football, Caleb found more than a game—he found a team, a dream, and a way to bond with his dad that would last a lifetime.

Caleb had been told about the importance of hard work, but now he was witnessing firsthand that with hardwork and dedication, anything is possible. He was living his dream and had found his passion in football.

As the days turned into weeks, Caleb's love for football only grew stronger. He practiced hard, played with friends, taught his dad a few moves, challenged his dad to Madden, and watched football on TV with his dad.

"Dad, thank you for allowing me to try out for the football team. I was a little scared to leave Chicago behind but now I'm excited to see what else this place might have in store," Caleb said with a smile.

"You are going to be special at whatever you do in life. Just know that I've got your back," his dad replied, his heart filled with love.

As the sun set on the Crescent City skyline, Caleb's heart soared with gratitude and excitement for the many adventures yet to come.

The Bright Broncos would go undefeated with a record of 14-0 and ultimately win the Johnny Bright Playground Championship.